ONCE ON THIS ISLAND

Photography © 1990 Martha Swope

Contents

About The Writers

LYNN AHRENS (Lyricist/Bookwriter) and STEPHEN FLAHERTY (Composer) have been collaborators in the musical theatre since 1983. Their musical farce "LUCKY STIFF" won the 1988 Richard Rodgers Production Award, and was produced Off-Broadway in 1988 by Playwrights Horizons. "LUCKY STIFF" was awarded Washington's 1990 Helen Hayes Award as Best Musical for its subsequent production at the Olney Theatre. Ahrens and Flaherty have also written for Theatreworks USA.

"ONCE ON THIS ISLAND" was first produced by Playwrights Horizons in 1990, directed and choreographed by Graciela Daniele. It opened to rave reviews in May of 1990, was named one of the Year's Ten Best Plays by the Burns Mantle Yearbook and was nominated for Best Musical by the New York Drama Critics Circle. It reopened the same year at the Booth Theatre on Broadway. The original cast album is available on RCA Victor. Currently, Ahrens and Flaherty are at work on the score for a new musical, "MY FAVORITE YEAR", an adaptation of the movie by the same name.

Individually, Ms. Ahrens is a four-time Emmy nominee for her work as a television writer, composer and lyricist and she won an Emmy Award for the ABC show "H.E.L.P." Her songs have been a mainstay of the renowned animated series "SCHOOLHOUSE ROCK". She is a graduate of The Newhouse School of Journalism at Syracuse University.

Mr. Flaherty is a graduate of Cincinnati College – Conservatory of Music, and did graduate work at New York University.

Ahrens and Flaherty have been the recipients of an NEA Producer's Grant, a National Institute for Music Theatre Award and an "AT&T New Plays for the Nineties" grant for "ONCE ON THIS ISLAND". They are both members of the Dramatists Guild.

WE DANCE

Words By
LYNN AHRENS

Music By
STEPHEN FLAHERTY

WAITING FOR LIFE

Words By
LYNN AHRENS

Music By
STEPHEN FLAHERTY

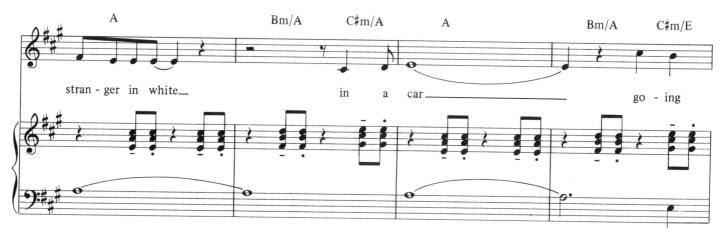

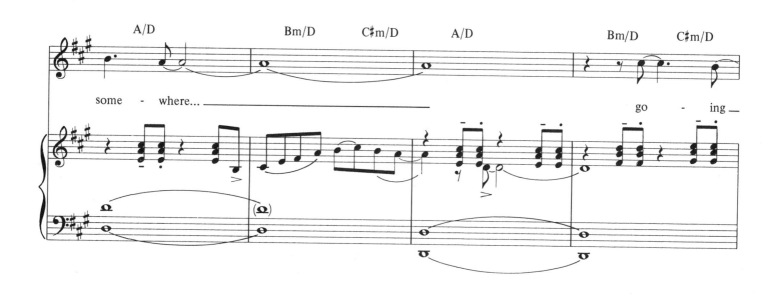

tell me to wait.___ Well, I'm wait - ing ___

wait - ing for life to be - gin! ___

Wait - ing for life to be - gin! ___

RAIN

Words By
LYNN AHRENS

Music By
STEPHEN FLAHERTY

FOREVER YOURS

Words By
LYNN AHRENS

Music By
STEPHEN FLAHERTY

Moderato, flowing

Sure as a wave needs to be near the shore,

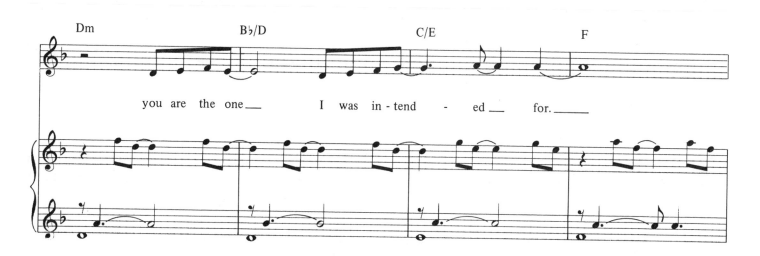

you are the one I was in-tend-ed for.

TI MOUNE

Words by
LYNN AHRENS

Music by
STEPHEN FLAHERTY

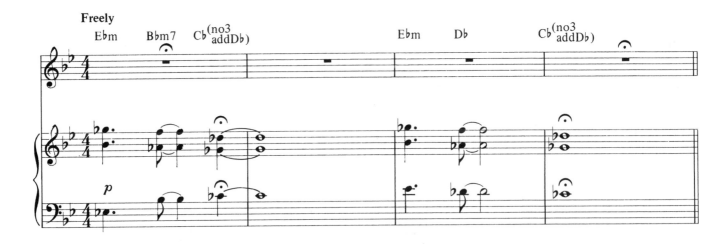

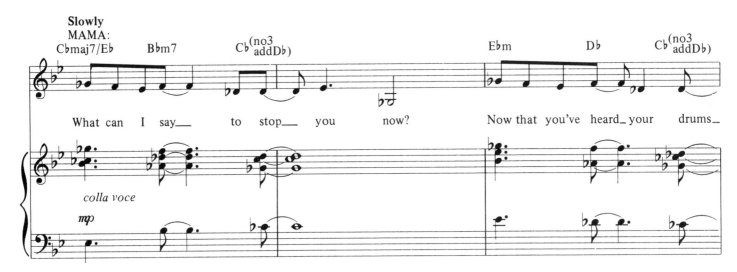

TI MOUNE:

with movement

What I am, you made me. What you gave, I owe. But if I look back, I'll nev-er go...

Who knows how high those moun-tains climb?

Who knows how deep these ri-vers flow? I knows he's there.

MAMA WILL PROVIDE

Words by
LYNN AHRENS

Music by
STEPHEN FLAHERTY

Bright calypso beat

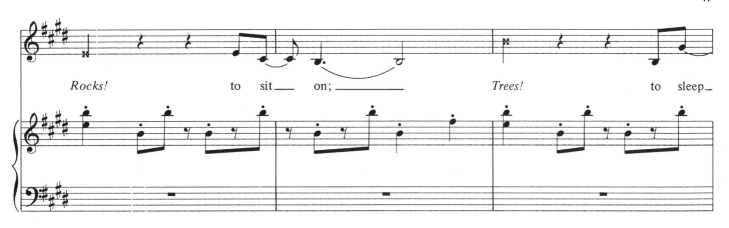

Rocks! to sit___ on; _____ *Trees!* to sleep___

___ un - der - neath; *Sand!* fun___ for your toes;___ *Plan -*

tain! to fill up your bel - ly; _____ *Breeze!* to fan___ your face;___

___ *Grass!* for mak - ing your bed;___ *Mos -*

THE HUMAN HEART

Words by
LYNN AHRENS

Music by
STEPHEN FLAHERTY

SOME GIRLS

Words by
LYNN AHRENS

Music by
STEPHEN FLAHERTY

Some girls___ take hours___ to paint ev - 'ry per - fect___

Gmaj7　　　　　Cmaj7　　　　　F♯

You're no one else I've known...

sub. p

D　　　　E/F♯

Some girls＿＿ take plea - sure ＿＿ in

p

D/G　　　　A　　G/A　　D　　　　D/F♯

buy - ing a fine trous - seau,＿＿＿＿＿＿＿

G　　　　G/A　　A　　D　　　　E/F♯

count - ing＿＿ each trea - sure and

ty - ing each ti - ny___ bow._____

___ They fold up their fu - tures with

per - fumed___ hands, while you face___ the fu - ture___ with

no de - mands.___ Some girls___ ex - pect things

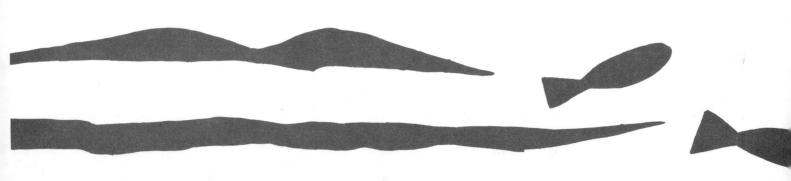

CAST
(in alphabetical order)

The Storytellers:

Daniel . . . . JERRY DIXON

Erzulie, Goddess of Love . . . . ANDREA FRIERSON

Mama Euralie . . . . SHEILA GIBBS

Ti Moune . . . . LA CHANZE

Asaka, Mother of the Earth . . . . KECIA LEWIS-EVANS

Little Ti Moune . . . . AFI McCLENDON

Armand . . . . GERRY McINTYRE

Agwe, God of Water . . . . MILTON CRAIG NEALY

Andrea . . . . NIKKI RENE

Papa Ge, Demon of Death . . . . ERIC RILEY

Tonton Julian . . . . ELLIS E. WILLIAMS

Place:

An island in the French Antilles

Time:

Night, in a storm

UNDERSTUDIES

Understudies never substitute for listed players unless a specific announcement
for the appearance is made at the time of the performance.
For Mama Euralie, Ti Moune, Asaka, Andrea — Fuschia Walker; for Erzulie — Nikki Rene;
for Daniel, Armand, Tonton Julian — Keith Tyrone; for Agwe, Papa Ge — Gerry McIntyre.